MY
MILLION
DOLLAR
IDEAS
JOURNAL

WELCOME TO YOUR NEW MILLION DOLLAR IDEAS JOURNAL

This is a place for you to write down your **million dollar ideas** and to prime your brain to being open and receptive to all the opportunities that are around you, on a daily basis.

Write down the **date**, what your **idea** is, the **type of idea** it is (e.g. digital product, service, property, or tangible goods etc) and its **difficulty level**.

Of course most ideas will be difficult or everyone would be doing it. Aim for the most simple idea, they're often the best.

Then detail any thoughts about your idea, its challenges, any potential supporters who might help you take it further.

Also consider who your idea will benefit. Does it contribute to a greater good or solve a problem? It should...

Here is where to let your creativity flow!

OK!

ARE YOU READY?

THEN, LET'S GET GOING!

Date:	
Idea/Type:	
Difficulty Level:	

NOTES

Date:	
Idea/Type:	
Difficulty Level:	

NOTES

_____
_____
_____
_____
_____
_____
_____
_____
_____
_____
_____
_____
_____
_____
_____
_____
_____
_____
_____
_____
_____

Date:

Idea/Type:

Difficulty Level:

NOTES

Date:
Idea/Type:
Difficulty Level:

NOTES

Date:
Idea/Type:
Difficulty Level:

NOTES

Date:	
Idea/Type:	
Difficulty Level:	

NOTES

_____

_____

_____

_____

_____

_____

_____

_____

_____

_____

_____

_____

_____

_____

_____

_____

_____

_____

_____

_____

_____

| Date: |
| Idea/Type: |
| Difficulty Level: |

NOTES

_____
_____
_____
_____
_____
_____
_____
_____
_____
_____
_____
_____
_____
_____
_____
_____
_____
_____
_____
_____
_____
_____
_____

| Date: |
| Idea/Type: |
| Difficulty Level: |

NOTES

_____
_____
_____
_____
_____
_____
_____
_____
_____
_____
_____
_____
_____
_____
_____
_____
_____
_____
_____
_____
_____
_____

Date:	
Idea/Type:	
Difficulty Level:	

NOTES

Date:
Idea/Type:
Difficulty Level:

NOTES

| Date: |
| Idea/Type: |
| Difficulty Level: |

NOTES

Date:

Idea/Type:

Difficulty Level:

NOTES

Date:
Idea/Type:
Difficulty Level:

NOTES

Date:

Idea/Type:

Difficulty Level:

NOTES

| Date: |
| Idea/Type: |
| Difficulty Level: |

NOTES

_____

_____

_____

_____

_____

_____

_____

_____

_____

_____

_____

_____

_____

_____

_____

_____

_____

_____

_____

_____

_____

Date:	
Idea/Type:	
Difficulty Level:	

NOTES

_____
_____
_____
_____
_____
_____
_____
_____
_____
_____
_____
_____
_____
_____
_____
_____
_____
_____
_____
_____
_____
_____

Date:	
Idea/Type:	
Difficulty Level:	

NOTES

Date:	
Idea/Type:	
Difficulty Level:	

NOTES

| Date: |
| Idea/Type: |
| Difficulty Level: |

NOTES

_____
_____
_____
_____
_____
_____
_____
_____
_____
_____
_____
_____
_____
_____
_____
_____
_____
_____
_____
_____
_____
_____

Date:

Idea/Type:

Difficulty Level:

NOTES

| Date: |
| Idea/Type: |
| Difficulty Level: |

NOTES

Date:	
Idea/Type:	
Difficulty Level:	

NOTES

_____

_____

_____

_____

_____

_____

_____

_____

_____

_____

_____

_____

_____

_____

_____

_____

_____

_____

_____

_____

Date:

Idea/Type:

Difficulty Level:

NOTES

| Date: |
| Idea/Type: |
| Difficulty Level: |

NOTES

Date:

Idea/Type:

Difficulty Level:

NOTES

| Date: |
| Idea/Type: |
| Difficulty Level: |

NOTES

Date:	
Idea/Type:	
Difficulty Level:	

NOTES

_____

_____

_____

_____

_____

_____

_____

_____

_____

_____

_____

_____

_____

_____

_____

_____

_____

_____

_____

_____

_____

| Date: |
| Idea/Type: |
| Difficulty Level: |

NOTES

Date:

Idea/Type:

Difficulty Level:

NOTES

Date:
Idea/Type:
Difficulty Level:

NOTES

Date:

Idea/Type:

Difficulty Level:

NOTES

_____

_____

_____

_____

_____

_____

_____

_____

_____

_____

_____

_____

_____

_____

_____

_____

_____

_____

_____

_____

_____

_____

_____

Date:
Idea/Type:
Difficulty Level:

NOTES

Date:

Idea/Type:

Difficulty Level:

NOTES

Date:	
Idea/Type:	
Difficulty Level:	

NOTES

Date:	
Idea/Type:	
Difficulty Level:	

NOTES

_____
_____
_____
_____
_____
_____
_____
_____
_____
_____
_____
_____
_____
_____
_____
_____
_____
_____
_____
_____
_____

Date:

Idea/Type:

Difficulty Level:

NOTES

Date:	
Idea/Type:	
Difficulty Level:	

NOTES

_____

_____

_____

_____

_____

_____

_____

_____

_____

_____

_____

_____

_____

_____

_____

_____

_____

_____

_____

| Date: |
| Idea/Type: |
| Difficulty Level: |

NOTES

_____

_____

_____

_____

_____

_____

_____

_____

_____

_____

_____

_____

_____

_____

_____

_____

_____

_____

_____

_____

Date:
Idea/Type:
Difficulty Level:

NOTES

Date:
Idea/Type:
Difficulty Level:

NOTES

| Date: |
| Idea/Type: |
| Difficulty Level: |

NOTES

_____
_____
_____
_____
_____
_____
_____
_____
_____
_____
_____
_____
_____
_____
_____
_____
_____
_____
_____
_____
_____

Date:
Idea/Type:
Difficulty Level:

NOTES

_____
_____
_____
_____
_____
_____
_____
_____
_____
_____
_____
_____
_____
_____
_____
_____
_____
_____
_____
_____
_____

Date:

Idea/Type:

Difficulty Level:

NOTES

| **Date:** |
| **Idea/Type:** |
| **Difficulty Level:** |

NOTES

| Date: |
| Idea/Type: |
| Difficulty Level: |

NOTES

_____

_____

_____

_____

_____

_____

_____

_____

_____

_____

_____

_____

_____

_____

_____

_____

_____

_____

_____

_____

Date:

Idea/Type:

Difficulty Level:

NOTES

Date:	
Idea/Type:	
Difficulty Level:	

NOTES

Date:
Idea/Type:
Difficulty Level:

NOTES

Date:

Idea/Type:

Difficulty Level:

NOTES

Date:
Idea/Type:
Difficulty Level:

NOTES

Date:

Idea/Type:

Difficulty Level:

NOTES

_____

_____

_____

_____

_____

_____

_____

_____

_____

_____

_____

_____

_____

_____

_____

_____

_____

_____

| Date: |
| Idea/Type: |
| Difficulty Level: |

NOTES

_____

_____

_____

_____

_____

_____

_____

_____

_____

_____

_____

_____

_____

_____

_____

_____

_____

_____

_____

_____

_____

Date:
Idea/Type:
Difficulty Level:

NOTES

_____

_____

_____

_____

_____

_____

_____

_____

_____

_____

_____

_____

_____

_____

_____

_____

_____

_____

_____

| Date: |
| Idea/Type: |
| Difficulty Level: |

NOTES

Date:
Idea/Type:
Difficulty Level:

NOTES

Date:
Idea/Type:
Difficulty Level:

NOTES

_____

_____

_____

_____

_____

_____

_____

_____

_____

_____

_____

_____

_____

_____

_____

_____

_____

_____

_____

_____

Date:

Idea/Type:

Difficulty Level:

NOTES

| Date: |
| Idea/Type: |
| Difficulty Level: |

NOTES

_____

_____

_____

_____

_____

_____

_____

_____

_____

_____

_____

_____

_____

_____

_____

_____

_____

_____

_____

_____

_____

| Date: |
| Idea/Type: |
| Difficulty Level: |

NOTES

_____
_____
_____
_____
_____
_____
_____
_____
_____
_____
_____
_____
_____
_____
_____
_____
_____
_____
_____
_____
_____

Date:
Idea/Type:
Difficulty Level:

NOTES

Date:

Idea/Type:

Difficulty Level:

NOTES

Date:
Idea/Type:
Difficulty Level:

NOTES

Date:	
Idea/Type:	
Difficulty Level:	

NOTES

_____
_____
_____
_____
_____
_____
_____
_____
_____
_____
_____
_____
_____
_____
_____
_____
_____
_____
_____
_____
_____

Date:
Idea/Type:
Difficulty Level:

NOTES

Date:
Idea/Type:
Difficulty Level:

NOTES

Date:
Idea/Type:
Difficulty Level:

NOTES

| Date: |
| Idea/Type: |
| Difficulty Level: |

NOTES

| Date: |
| Idea/Type: |
| Difficulty Level: |

NOTES

_____
_____
_____
_____
_____
_____
_____
_____
_____
_____
_____
_____
_____
_____
_____
_____
_____
_____
_____
_____
_____

Date:

Idea/Type:

Difficulty Level:

NOTES

Date:	
Idea/Type:	
Difficulty Level:	

NOTES

Date:	
Idea/Type:	
Difficulty Level:	

NOTES

_____

_____

_____

_____

_____

_____

_____

_____

_____

_____

_____

_____

_____

_____

_____

_____

_____

_____

_____

_____

| Date: |
| Idea/Type: |
| Difficulty Level: |

NOTES

_____

_____

_____

_____

_____

_____

_____

_____

_____

_____

_____

_____

_____

_____

_____

_____

_____

_____

_____

_____

Date:	
Idea/Type:	
Difficulty Level:	

NOTES

| Date: |
| Idea/Type: |
| Difficulty Level: |

NOTES

Date:	
Idea/Type:	
Difficulty Level:	

NOTES

Date:
Idea/Type:
Difficulty Level:

NOTES

Date:
Idea/Type:
Difficulty Level:

NOTES

| Date: |
| Idea/Type: |
| Difficulty Level: |

NOTES

_____
_____
_____
_____
_____
_____
_____
_____
_____
_____
_____
_____
_____
_____
_____
_____
_____
_____
_____
_____
_____
_____

Date:

Idea/Type:

Difficulty Level:

NOTES

Date:

Idea/Type:

Difficulty Level:

NOTES

Date:

Idea/Type:

Difficulty Level:

NOTES

_____

_____

_____

_____

_____

_____

_____

_____

_____

_____

_____

_____

_____

_____

_____

_____

_____

_____

_____

_____

Date:
Idea/Type:
Difficulty Level:

NOTES

_____

_____

_____

_____

_____

_____

_____

_____

_____

_____

_____

_____

_____

_____

_____

_____

_____

_____

_____

_____

Date:

Idea/Type:

Difficulty Level:

NOTES

Date:
Idea/Type:
Difficulty Level:

NOTES

| Date: |
| Idea/Type: |
| Difficulty Level: |

NOTES

_____

_____

_____

_____

_____

_____

_____

_____

_____

_____

_____

_____

_____

_____

_____

_____

_____

_____

_____

_____

_____

| Date: |
| Idea/Type: |
| Difficulty Level: |

NOTES

Date:	
Idea/Type:	
Difficulty Level:	

NOTES

Date:
Idea/Type:
Difficulty Level:

NOTES

Date:	
Idea/Type:	
Difficulty Level:	

NOTES

Date:	
Idea/Type:	
Difficulty Level:	

NOTES

| Date: |
| Idea/Type: |
| Difficulty Level: |

NOTES

_____
_____
_____
_____
_____
_____
_____
_____
_____
_____
_____
_____
_____
_____
_____
_____
_____
_____
_____
_____
_____

Date:

Idea/Type:

Difficulty Level:

NOTES

_____
_____
_____
_____
_____
_____
_____
_____
_____
_____
_____
_____
_____
_____
_____
_____
_____
_____
_____
_____
_____

Date:

Idea/Type:

Difficulty Level:

NOTES

_____

_____

_____

_____

_____

_____

_____

_____

_____

_____

_____

_____

_____

_____

_____

_____

_____

_____

_____

Date:
Idea/Type:
Difficulty Level:

NOTES

| Date: |
| Idea/Type: |
| Difficulty Level: |

NOTES

Date:	
Idea/Type:	
Difficulty Level:	

NOTES

Date:
Idea/Type:
Difficulty Level:

NOTES

Well done idea creator!

You've reached the end of your million dollar ideas journal.

I hope one of these makes you a millionaire!

Good Luck!

Made in the USA
Las Vegas, NV
09 April 2021